Treasure of Kalidasa Series 05

RITU-SAMHARA
OR
AN ACCOUNT OF SEASONS

Treasure of Kalidasa Series 05

RITU-SAMHARA
OR
AN ACCOUNT OF SEASONS

[TRANSLATED INTO ENGLISH]

A POEM by

KALIDASA

PUBLISHED BY
THE SOCIETY FOR THE RESUSCITATION
OF INDIAN LITERATURE.

GYAN

Published by

GYAN

Gyan Publishing House
5, Ansari Road
Daryaganj, New Delhi-110002
Phone: 011-47034999, 9811692060
E-mail: books@gyanbooks.com

Distribution Network
gyanbooks.com
India, USA, Canada, UK, Australia, France

ISBN : 978-81-212-2449-9 (PB)
First Published, 1901

2nd Impression 2021

Printed at: Gyan Press, Delhi.

Treasure of Kalidasa Series 05
Ritu-Samhara or An Account of Seasons
Author: Kalidasa

RITU-SAMHARA

OR

AN ACCOUNT OF SEASONS.

[*TRANSLATED INTO ENGLISH*]

A POEM BY

KALIDASA.

PUBLISHED BY

THE SOCIETY FOR THE RESUSCITATION
OF INDIAN LITERATURE.

CALCUTTA:
PRINTED BY H. C. DAS, ELYSIUM PRESS,
Kashi Ghose's Lane, Beadon Street.

1901.

RITU SAMHARA.

A DESCRIPTION OF THE SUMMER.

O Dear, of late the Summer has set in when the rays of the sun become very fierce, the clear and cool rays of the moon are sought, the watery contents of big ponds become scanty for people continually bathing there and the force of Cupid becomes lessened.

During this season people are fond of moon-lit nights, water houses, various jewels and sandal-paste.

During summer nights seated at ease in sweet-scented and charming mansons men enjoy the nectar of lips shaken by the air of the mouth and sweet music of Vina set in tunes.

With waists decorated with chains, breasts pasted with sandal and bedecked with necklace, and tresses perfumed with charming scents beautiful damsels remove the summer sufferings of the males.

Dying their feet with deep red-dyes the beautiful waisted damsels beautify the Nupuras making sound sweet to the ears like swans. Their every foot-step increases the passion of men. Look, O dear, whose calm mind is not agitated with sentiments of love on seeing the rising breasts of damsels pasted with sandal, their breasts adorned with necklaces and their waists bedecked with golden chains?

Always perspiring heavily the youthful damsels, with pointed breasts, cast off thick-set clothes and cover their breasts with thin ones.

By means of the wind of fans soaked with sandal water, by means of touching the breasts, covered with necklaces of women and by the sweet music of Vina, even the sleeping sentiment of love in men's minds is excited.

Seeing the faces of women lying asleep in night at white mansions and chastising his own beauty, the moon, filled with shame, becomes pale in the morning.

The earth is stricken with the fierce heat of the sun, the dust is raised by the terrible wind. Even persons, living in strange countries and having their minds consumed by the fire of separation from their loves, cannot look at it.

Greatly assailed by the heat of the sun and with tongues dried up by thirst the deer are looking up to the blue sky mistaking it for a pond. The glances of sportive women, accompanied with smiles like unto the moon-lit night were creating desire in the minds of men living apart from their wives.

Assailed with excessive heat and scorched with the heated dust ; the serpents, sighing heavily, and with their hoods bent, are taking shelter under the shade of the peacock's feathers.

The lions have become weak and shorn of energy with thirst. They are breathing hard and lying on earth with their mouths wide open. Their tongues are shaking with thirst. Their manes are trembling. And even seeing the elephants near they are not rising up to kill them.

With their throats dried up with thirst, stricken with thirst and heat not getting even a drop of water they are running about hither and thither in search of it and are not terrified at seeing a lion.

The body and the mind of the peacocks have been greatly assailed with the fierce rays of the sun like unto fire increased by sacrificial offerings. Though the serpents are taking shelter under their tails they are not killing them.

Greatly assailed with heat the boars with their long mouths are digging the dried mud of the tanks as if they are seeking shelter in the nether region in search of cold water.

Assailed with heat the frogs are leaping up from heated and muddy water and are waiting under the fangs of snakes stricken with thirst.

Assailing one another and quarrelling amongst themselves the elephants are uprooting lotuses from the lake, killing the distressed fishes, driving away the terrified Sarasas and drying up the mud of the tank.

The jem, set on the hood of the serpents, is being lighted up with the rays of the sun. They are drinking air with their tongues. And distressed with the fire of their vemon, the heat of the sun and thirst they are not killing even the frogs.

From the trembling mouth of the buffaloes reddened tongues, covered with foams, are coming out. And stricken with thirst and seeking water with their faces turned up they are coming out of the mountain caves.

The green grass of the forest has been scorched by the forest-fire, dried leaves are being carried away by strong winds, the tanks are being dried up by the heat of the sun. To look to any side of the forest inspires one with fear.

Although a greater portion of leaves has fallen down from trees still sitting somehow on them the birds are breathing. Tired the monkeys are seeking the groves of the mountains. The Sarabhas with great difficulty are taking up water from the wells.

Increased by the wind, fire, red like red lead or new blown Kusuma flowers, is consuming the earth as if being anxious to embrace the tops of trees and creepers.

Forest-fire is being lighted and increased in mountain caves by the fierce wind, is with great sound entering into the forest of dried bamboos, is spreading on all sids in the midst of the heap of cotton and touching the hairs of the deer is killing them. Collected in a mass in the forest of Salmali trees, the fire, spreading its golden rays, is blowing in the cavity of trees. It is spreading up to its top on getting dried leaves and is moving about on all sides of the forest with the help of the wind,

Assailed with the forest-fire, elephants, Gavayas, and lions, forgetting their enmity and behaving towards one another as friends, are going out of the forest scorched with the fire and taking shelter on the banks of the rivers are entering into them.

Lotuses being unfolded in the lakes have put on a beautiful appearance and all the quarters have been perfumed with the smell of Patala flowers. At this time, plunging into cool water and clear rays of the moon are welcome unto people. The women and to listen to sweet songs in summer are objects of great enjoyment.

A DESCRIPTION OF THE RAINY SEASON.

O dear, with the infuriated elephants in the shape of clouds surcharged with water, with flags in the form of fightings and musical instruments in the shape of thunder, all favourite unto pleasure-seekers, the beautiful rainy season has appeared like a king.

Appearing somewhere like red lotus, somewhere

like ground collyrium and somewhere like breasts of pregnant women the clouds have covered the sky.

Pouring rain in torrents at the request of the thirst-stricken Chatakas and emitting slow mutterings pleasing to the ears, clouds, bent down by the weight of their watery contents, are slowly moving on.

Making sounds of music with thunder, taking rainbow with the string of lightning set to it and with the strokes of sharpened arrows in the shape of torrents the clouds are agitating the minds of people.

With green grass which have grown like Vaidurya jems riving the earth, leaves of Kandali creepers and Indragopa insects the earth has been filled up. It appears as if prostitutes, bedecked with red jems, are sitting there.

Maddened with joy the peacocks are emitting sweet notes. Sometimes they are unfolding their tails, sometimes showing anxiety to kiss and embrace their mates and are again dancing.

The rivers being filled up with the muddy water of the rains their force is increased. Therefore felling down the trees on both the banks, they, like unchaste women, are going quickly towards the ocean.

With tender green grass, remnants, after the deer have grazed on them, and with trees clothed with new leaves and branches the forests on the mount Vindhya are pilfering the minds of men.

The deer, endued with eyes like trembling Kuvalaya flowers are seeing the beauty of the forest with terror-stricken looks, and are exciting curiosity in the mind.

The clouds are always muttering dreadfully and have enshrouded the night with thick darkness. Still finding their way by the light of the lightning the unchaste women are going to their lovers.

Surprised at the deep muttering of clouds and flashes of lightning the women are embracing again and again their offending husbands on the bed.

Sprinkling their lips with the water from their Kuvalaya-like eyes, and casting aside garlands, ornaments, scents etc., objects of enjoyments, the wives of absentee husbands are spending the night in despair.

Terrified at seeing the new water spoiled with insects, grass and other refuges the frogs are going down obliquely like snakes.

Leaving the full-blown lotuses, anxious to give honey, in expectation of new ones the insensible black-bees, humming sweetly, are sitting on the feathers of dancing peacoks mistaking them for lotuses.

The infuriated wild elephants are crying again and again at the muttering of new clouds. The black-bees are covering their temples for temporal juice.

Clouds, bent down by the weight of water, are overing all the sides of the mountain. The fountains are filled with water and the peacocks are dancing in delight. With these objects of beauty the mountains are filling the minds if men with curiosity.

Whose mind is not being maddened by the breeze cooled by coming in contact with clouds surcharged with water, shaking the Kadamva, Sarja, Arjuna, Neepa and Ketaki trees and spreading the perfume of their flowers?

Spreading their tresses up to their waist and decorating their ears with sweet-scented flowers, the women, showing their breasts adorned with necklaces and faces smelling liquor, are exciting lust in the mind of lustful men.

The clouds, bent down by the weight of water and accompanied with lightnings and rain-bows and the women, adorned with jewelled waist-bands and ear-rings, are simultaneously agitating the minds of men living apart from their wives.

Making garlands of sweet scented Ketaki, Kadamva and Keshara flowers and making ear-rings with the filaments of Arjuna flowers the pleasure-seeking women are decorating their heads and ears.

Perfuming their person with black Aguru sandal, putting on ear-rings of flowers and binding their tresses, the women, on hearing the muttering of clouds in the evening, are quickly leaving the apartments of their elders for their own bed-rooms.

Shaken slowly by the breeze, the clouds, black like red lotuses, huge, bent down by water and adorned with lightnings and rain-bows, are pelfering the minds of women having travelling husbands.

The heat of the forest has been removed by the sprinkling of new water and the Kadamva flowers have blossomed. It appears that the forest is experiencing horripillation out of joy. On the branches of trees being shaken by the wind it appears that the entire forest is dancing in delight. On the blossoming of Ketaka flowers it appears that the forest is smiling.

Like unto a husband this rainy season has put on the heads of women garlands of Malati, Yuthika Vakula and other full blown wild flowers, and ear-rings of Kadamva flowers on their ears.

During this season the women carry chains on their rising breasts, thick clothes on their waists, and tresses of hairs accompanied with drops of perspiration caused by their watering the plants, on the middle part of their body.

Beholding the beauty of trees pressed down by flowers soaked with drops of new rain in this season and with the scent of Ketaki flowers the women are worked up with joy.

Thinking "He is our refuge when we are bent down by the weight of water" the clouds are enliveing with torrents the mount Vindhya assailed with fierce heat (of the summer.)

O dear, may the rainy season, the pilferer of the heart of many a beautiful women, the sincere friend of trees and creepers and the life of creatures, do you good ever and anon.

A DESCRIPTION OF THE AUTUMN.

Clothed in a raiment of kasa flowers, and making a sound of *nupuras* in the shape of the cries of maddened geese, the lotus-faced and the highly beautiful autumn has appeared like a newly wedded bride. Ripe paddies on all sides are appearing like her beautiful limbs.

In this season the earth has been whitened with kasa flowers, the night with the moon, the river with the swans and the lakes with Malati flowers.

Having fckle and beautiful Shaphari fishes for their tongues, the rows of swans sitting on their banks for neck-chains and the extensive banks for their waists the rivers are flowing slowly like inebriete women.

Some where white like a conch or a lotus and fanned by cloud-like chowries, passing in hundred parts on being thinned by the pouring of water and shaken by the wind the sky is shining like a king.

What youth is there whose mind is not attracted by this autumn in which the sky is beautiful like a mass of ground collyruim, the earth is sunny with Banduka flowers and the waters are covered with beautiful lotuses ?

The maddened black-bees are drinking the honey of kovidar trees, whose charming branches are being slowly shaken by the soft breeze and covered with tender leaves abounding in profuse flowers. Who is there, whose mind is not rent asunder by this spectacle?

Clad in a raiment of clear rays and adorned with ornaments of stars, the moon-faced night, setting aside the veil of clouds is increasing day by day like a girl.

The waves of the rivers are being broken by Karandavas. The banks are being covered with swans and Sarasas and the filaments of lotuses and the swans are emitting notes hither and hither. Whose mind is not delighted with seeing these beautiful sights?

Adorned with rays giving joy to the eyes and stealing away minds, the dew-powing moon, ever producing delight of the mind, is assailing the persons of women assailed with the poisonous shafts of the death of their husbands.

Shaking the paddy creepers bent down with the weight of fruits, making the Karuvaka trees pressed down with the weight of flowers dance and shaking the full blown lotuses the wind is by force agitating the mind of young men.

Adorned with the pairs of maddened swans, pure and full blown lotuses and lillies, the lakes, in which waves have been caused by the soft morning breeze, are agitating suddenly the mind of all.

The rainbow has disappeared in the clouds, the lightnings do not appear on the flag of the sky, the cranes do not shake the sky with the wind of their wings and the peacocks do not look up to the sky.

Leaving the peacocks who have desisted from dancing Kamadeva is approaching the swans emitting sweet notes, and leaving aside the kadamwa, Surja, Arjuna and Neepa trees is going to Saptachada trees.

The gardens have been beautified with Shephetika flowers. Residing there the birds are emiting sweet notes with great glee. The eyes of the she-deer, living in the forest skirts, are looking like lotuses. Seeing these sights the minds of men are being greatly agitated.

Trembling the forests of kalhara, lotus and lillies, becoming cooler in their contact and carrying dews placed on leaves the morning breeze is creating great agitation.

Covered with ripe paddy, beautified with kine grazing at ease and echoing with the notes of swans and Sarasas, the fields, situate on the village skirts, are gladdening the people.

The swans are imitating the charming gait of women, the full blown lotuses the beauty of their face, the red lotuses their beautiful glances and the waves the charming gestures of their eye-brows.

The leaves of Shyama creepers, bent down by the weight of flowers, are imitating the beauty of the adorned gems of women and the garlands of Asoka flowers that of their smiles beautifying their lips.

The women are decorating their dark-blue tresses with new Malati flowers and putting on various red lotuses on their ears adorned with most excellent golden ear-rings.

Filled with great delight the women are decorating their breasts with chain soaked in Sandal paste, their capacious waists with Rasana chains and their feet with Nupuras making sweet sound.

During this autumn the moon, freed from clouds, the sky bespangled with stars and the lakes covered with full blown lillies, adorned with swans and water clear like emerald are appearing highly beautiful. Cooled by coming in contact with flowers the breeze blows in autumn. The quarters are freed of clouds and delightful. The earth is freed of mud. The sky is adorned with clear rays of the moon and garland of stars.

In the morning of this season, the lotuses, unfolded by the rays of the sun, put on the beauty of the most youthful damsel. When the rays of the moon disappear the lillies fade away like the smiles of women whose husbands are away.

Seeing the beauty of their wives' eyes in red lotuses, the beauty of their sounding gold ornaments in mad swans, the beauty of their cheeks in Banduka flowers, the travellers weep with their minds greatly agitated.

Transferring the beauty of the moon to the countenances of women, the notes of the geese to the Nupuras, the beauty of Badhuka flowers to the lips the beautiful autumn is as if disappering.

May this season autumn, with a countenance like a full blown lotus, with eyes like red lotuses, clothed in blossoming Kasa flowers like unto a white raiment, and smiling like lillies, give in profusion joy to your minds like an inebriete damsel.

A DESCRIPTION OF HEMANTA OR THE DEWY SEASON.

O dear, the Hemanta has set in. In this season the herbs have become beautiful with the growth of new leaves, the Lodhra trees have blossomed, the paddy has rippened, the lotus is being blown up and heavy dews are falling.

The breasts of women, having beautiful breasts, are not being dyed with red arsenic and the snow is not being decorated with Kunda flowers and moon-like garlands of pearls.

Bangles and ornaments are not finding room on the hands and arms of women and thin cloth is not finding room on their waist and breasts.

The damsels are not decorating their waists with

chains of gold set with jems and their lotus feet with Nupuras.

For celebrating the festival of sexual intercourse the women are dying their bodies with turmeric, decorating their lotus-like countenances with leaves and perfuming their heads with black Aguru and incense.

The countenances of women have become weak and pale with the toil of sexual intercourse; on account of growing joy they are not laughing aloud on seeing lips wounded with teeth.

The winter has occupied the breasts and thighs of women. And being weakened by their oppressions they are weeping in the morning with tears falling in the shape of dews from leaves.

The boundary lines, being covered with profuse paddy beautified with the she-deer and resonant with cries of beautiful Krounchas moving about on all sides, are gladdening the minds of the people.

Adorned with full blown red lotuses, maddened geese and clear water, the cool lakes are pilfering the hearts of men.

O dear, the Priyangu creepers are being continually shaken by the breeze, cooled by snow, riping and looking pale like women stricken with the absence of their husbands.

The mouths of men are being perfumed by drinking the honey of flowers and their persons are being scented with breaths. Desirous of holding sexual intercourse they are lying down embracing each other.

The merciless sexual intercourse of youthful damsels has manifested itself in the lips marked with cuts of teeth and breasts wounded with nails.

Some women, holding up mirrors, are decorating their lotus faces in the new beams of the sun and biting their lips already bitten by their lovers.

Some woman has been greatly exhausted with the toil of sexual intercourse. Her eyes have become reddened with night-keeping. And keeping her scattered hairs on the end of the bed and being heated by the mild rays of the sun she is sleeping.

Another woman, looking beautiful with her black tresses, and pressed down with the weight of her rising breasts, is dressing her hairs, removing therefrom the garlands used before the sweet scent whereof has disappeared.

Seeing her own person enjoyed by her lover and accordingly filled with delight another youthful damsel is increasing the beauty of her lips. Drawing her hairs for binding them into tresses she is contracting a little her eye-brows. And she is putting on a new cloth. Some beautiful damsels have been greatly worn out with the toil of sexual intercourse. Their limbs have been exhausted and their capacious thighs and breasts have swollen. They are rubbing their persons with sweet-scented oil and turmeric.

The boundaries of the villages have been covered

with ripe paddies. May this Hemanta, the mine of many virtues, the pilferers of the hearts of charming women and reasonant with the notes of kraunchas, conduce to your happiness.

A DESCRIPTION OF THE WINTER.

O thou of most excellent thighs, listen to an account of the winter when the earth is covered with paddy and sugar-candy, when the Krounchas emit notes at their sweet pleasure and when all sorts of enjoyments attain to their consummation—the winter which is favourite unto women.

In this season, rooms with windows closed, fire, the rays of the sun and women clad in thick clothes are the objects of enjoyment unto men.

Sandal, cool like the rays of the moon, the roof of mansions, clear like the autumnal moon, breeze cooled by snow cannot attract the mind of men in this season.

In this season people do not like places cool with the fall of dews and the night cooled with the rays of the moon and adorned with stars.

Eating betel leaves in great anxiety, wearing pastes and garlands and perfuming their faces with the honey of flowers the women are entering into bed rooms sufficiently perfumed with black Aguru.

Beholding their husbands, offending, trembling and scolded the women, inebriete with drinking honey, are forgetting their previous offences being desirous of holding sexual intercourse. Being kept up till late hours by cruel youths engaged in sexual intercourse these youthful damsels, with their breasts perspiring, walk slowly in the morning.

With their breasts adorned with beautiful filaments, waists clad in silken raiments and tresses bedecked with flowers the damsels are beautifying the, more the winter.

Rendered twany by the red arsenic dyes of women and pressed and protected by their enjoyable breasts the source of heat the lustful persons are sleeping at ease after defeating the winter.

In winter nights filled with delight women drink, in the company of their husbands, most excellent wines, shaken by the sweet-scented breath and capable of creating exhilaration and desire.

Seeing, after the intoxication is over, her own person enjoyed by her lover some one amongst women, with breasts pressed down by the embrace of her dearest, is leaving smilingly her sleeping apartment for another room.

With fading garlands sweet-scented with Aguru and dishevelled curling locks some one, having capacious waist, deep navel and of a middle stature, is leaving in the morning her bed-chamber for another room. Adorned with eyes beautiful like golden lotuses, extending up to ears, washed immediately with water and having their extremities reddened, as well as with countenances with tresses hanging on the shoulders, some women are appearing highly beautiful in their rooms in the morning.

Pained with the weight of their capacious backs and as well as with that of their rising breasts some women are going slowly; and casting off their night dresses they are putting on those fit to be worn during the day.

Marking the disfigurement of their breasts caused by the hands and nails of their lovers, and paleness of their lips, cheeks and faces caused by kisses and teeth, during sexual intercourse in the night some women are hiding themselves in the room out of shame.

During this season molasses, Shaly padies and sugar canes are produced in abundance. Desire for enjoyments and luxuries increases and therefore the minds of those whose lovers are away are greatly agitated. O dear, may this winter conduce to your well being always.

A DESCRIPTION OF THE SPRING.

O dear, having mangoe blossoms for his sharp arrows and black bees for the string of his bow, the foremost of heroes Basanta (Spring) has come for rending the hearts of pleasure-seeking persons.

Now the trees are covered with flowers, the lakes are full of lotuses, the women are anxious for enjoyments, the wind is full of perfume, the winds are delightful and the days are beautiful. O dear, everything is beautiful during the spring.

This highly charming spring multiplies the beauty of the water of the lakes, of the jewelled girdle, of the lunar rays, of women and of mangoe trees bent down by blossoms.

During the spring the pleasure-seeking women, increase the beauty of their waists, with their raiments colored with Kusamba flowers and that of their breasts with those colored with red arsenic.

The beauty of full blown Mallika flowers is manifest in new Karnikara flowers serving for the ear-rings of women and in Asoka flowers decorating their black and curling locks.

They have put on their breasts chains pasted with white sandal, on their arms armlets, on their hands bracelets and on their waists girdles.

Drops of perspiration on the breasts and faces of women, resembling golden lotuses and adorned with sandal marks, are appearing like pearls born on their limbs.

Raiments are dropping down from their limbs assailed by the lovers with their enjoyments. And when they are approaching them the women are anxious to embrace them.

The limbs of the women have become weak and pale with sexual intercourse, anxious thoughts and night-keeping. They are sighing again and again in idleness. Ananga (Cupid) is making women (even in this plight) anxious to decorate their bodies and engage in enjoyments.

Kama is living in may forms on the persons of women—in their eyes worn out with intoxication, in their fickleness, in paleness of their breasts, in the depth of their navels, and spaciousness of their backs.

Ananga has made the limbs of women exhausted with night-keeping, has caused faltering in their speech with the drinking of wine and brought about the contraction of their eye-brows.

The damsels, exhausted with intoxication, are pasting their limbs and breasts with Pryangu, black aguru, red arsenic and sandal scented with musk.

Casting off thick raiments, men, pierced by the shafts of Kandarpa, are putting on dyed clothes perfumed with black Aguru.

The male coels, maddened with drinking the honey of mangoe blossoms, are kissing with joy their mates. Humming sweetly the black-bees, intent on drinking the honey of lotuses, are enlivening their dear ones.

The mango trees have been bent down a little with the weight of new red leaves. And blossoming their branches have put on a beautiful appearance. Shaken by the wind these mango trees are agitating the minds of women.

Covered up to roots with flowers dark-blue like lotus the blossoming Asoka trees are exciting the sorrow of separation in the minds of women.

Seeing the maddened black-bees kiss the beautiful flowers of the Madhavi creepers adorned with tender leaves shaken slowly by the breeze the minds of pleasure-seeking men are worked up with desire.

Who is there a conscious man whose mind is not pained with the arrows of Kandarpa on seeing the grace of the new grown blossoms of Kuruvaka trees pilfering the beauty of the faces of their dear wives.

With the advent of the spring the trees are being slowly shaken by the breeze. Adorned all over with the forests of Asoka trees bent down with flowers resembling burning fire the earth is looking like a forest damsel clad in a crimson coloured raiment.

Are not the hearts of young men and women rent asunder by the blossoming Kinsuka flowers crooked like the eyes of Shuka birds? Are they not scorched by the Karnikara flowers? Again the coels are killing them completely with their sweet notes.

Even the minds of bashful and gentle women of good families are being agitated in the spring by the notes of joyous coels and the humming of black-bees.

In the spring, with the termination of the winter, the slow and sweet breeze, shaking the blossoming branches of mango trees, spreading on all sides the notes of coels, is blowing pilfering the hearts of men.

Beautiful gardens, adorned with Kunda flowers white like the smiles of damsels, are stealing away even the minds of the ascetics shorn of the desire for enjoyment. They have already pilfered the minds of young men, stained with the desire for worldly enjoyments.

With golden girdles hanging on their waists and necklaces adorning their rising breasts the pleasure-seeking women, with the help of the notes of coels and black-bees, are pilfering the minds of men in the month of Chaitra.

Beholding the mountains, adorned with various blossoming trees and resonant with the notes of coels men are experiencing great delight.

Seeing the blossoming mango trees the traveller, with his mind stricken with separation from his dear wife, is opening his eyes, weeping, expressing sorrow, covering his nose with his hand and exclaiming cries of despair.

With the humming of black-bees inebriete with honey, notes of Kokilas, mango blossoms and charming Karnikara-like arrows the spring is continually wounding the hearts of sensitive women.

With beautiful mango blossoms for his arrows, Kingsuka flowers for his bow, black-bees for his bow-string, the moon for his umbrella, the southern wind for his infuriated elephant and the coels for his panegyrists may the god Kama, with his companion Spring, do good unto all.

In the spring the women perfume even the palaces oooled a little with frost with beautiful flowers and decorate their breasts with various flower garlands.

Seeing on the road mango trees like unto gold shaken by the breeze, pouring flowers, the travellers, whose weak body is not worthy of being struck, are swooning away being wounded with the shafts of Madana.

The spring is mocking at the sweet words of women by the sweet notes of the Kokilas, at their smiling teeth by the beauty of Kunda flowers and at their palms by new grown leaves.

With their charming, pale and lotus-like countenances resembling golden lotuses, with breasts pasted with sandal and decorated with necklace, and with inebriete glances the women are creating desire even in the minds of self-controlled Munis.

Of the lotus-like countenances perfumed with honey, of women, their eyes reddened a little like Lodhra flowers, beautiful tresses like Kuruvaka flowers, rising breasts and waists which is it that does not excite desire in the spring?

In this season even the firm-minded women are being worked up by the breeze perfumed with mango blossoms, and assailed by the notes of Kokilas and the humming of black-bees.

The charming evening, clear lunar rays, notes of male coels, the sweet scented breeze, the humming of maddened black-bees, and drinking in the night—all these excite the desire.

In this season men love shade of the trees in the day and the rays of the moon in the night. They lie down in cool mansions and embrace their lady loves.

THE END.